Beast ACADEMY

By Art of Problem Solving

MATH GUIDE
2B

Jason Batterson

Erich Owen

Published by: AoPS Incorporated
                    10865 Rancho Bernardo Rd Ste 100
                    San Diego, CA 92127-2102
                    info@BeastAcademy.com

ISBN: 978-1-934124-32-1

Written by Jason Batterson
Illustrated by Erich Owen
Additional Illustrations by Paul Cox
Colored by Greta Selman

Visit the Beast Academy website at BeastAcademy.com.
Visit the Art of Problem Solving website at artofproblemsolving.com.
Printed in the United States of America.
2018 Printing.

Become a Math Beast!
For additional books,
printables, and more, visit

BeastAcademy.com

This is Guide 2B in a four-book series:

Now Available!
Beast Academy Online

Learn more at BeastAcademy.com

Contents:

Alex
"The Executive"

IrOns his sOcks
Only wears
them tO bed

GrOgg (me!)

I can write with My feet! (nOt as well as with my hands)

Winnie
"The Firecracker"

Testy at times

DOn't be fOOled
by her
cüte handwriting

Lizzie
"The BOOkwOrm"

Read all 52 bOOks
in the DragOn Diaries
series

wrOte new endings
fOr 3 Of them

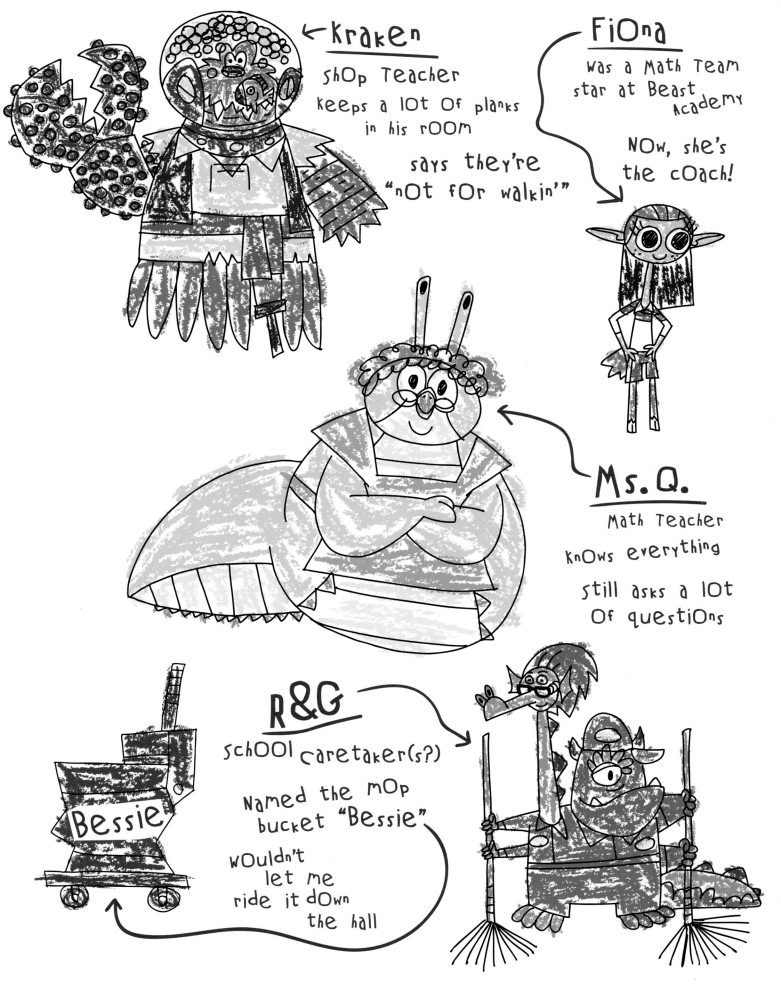

The Headmaster
How to use this book

Welcome to Beast Academy!

This book is called the Guide.

There is also a separate Practice book with lots of problems you can use to sharpen your skills.

The Guide is written like a comic book.

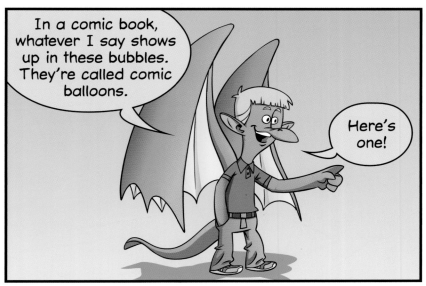

In a comic book, whatever I say shows up in these bubbles. They're called comic balloons.

Here's one!

Each character has a different balloon color. This makes it easy to tell who is talking.

My balloons are purple!

The story is told in panels.

Panels usually have a rectangular frame around them...

...like this one.

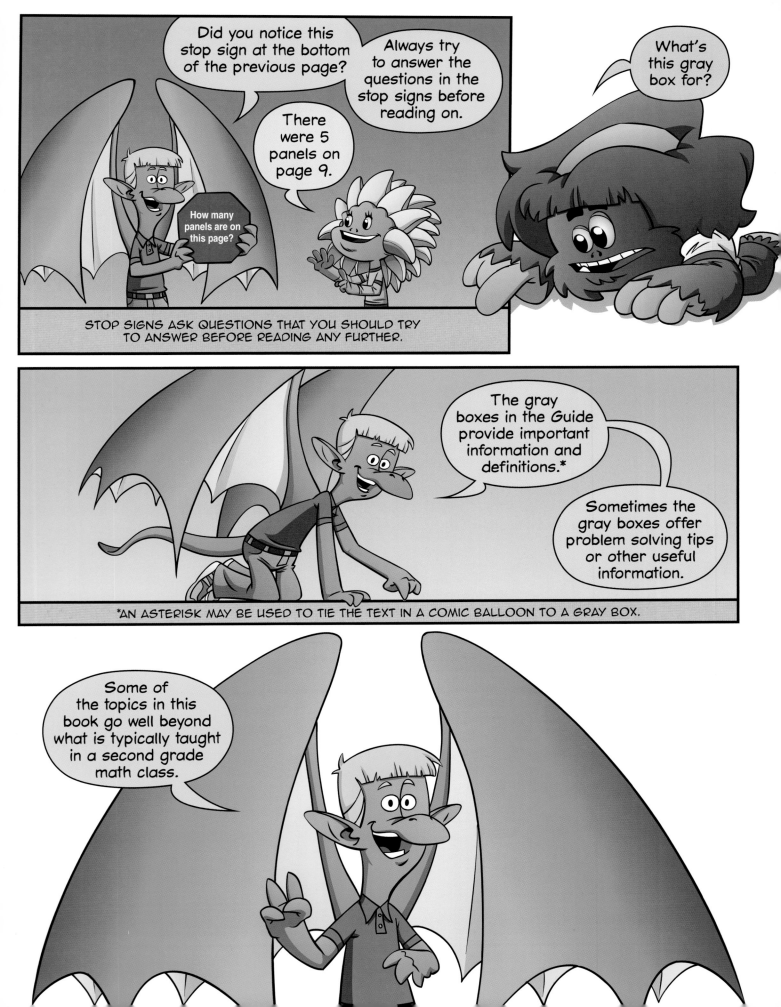

Contents: Chapter 4

See page 6 in the Practice book for a recommended reading/practice sequence for Chapter 4.

Chapter 4:
Subtraction

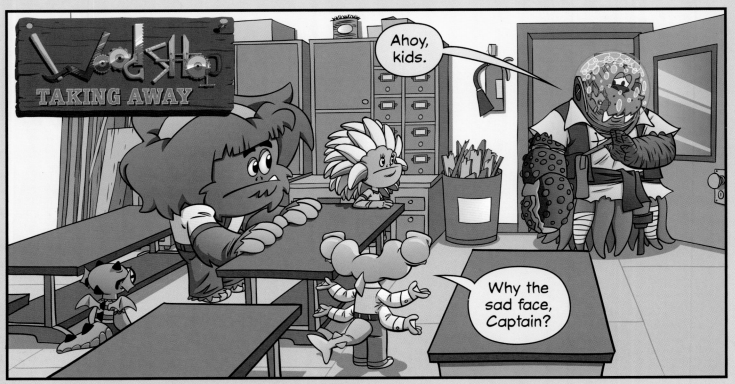

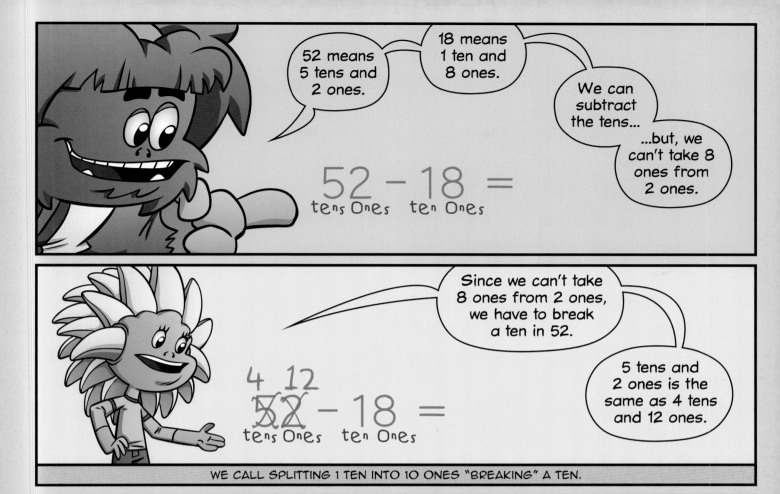

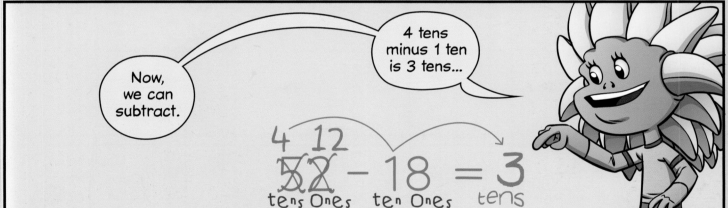

WE CALL SPLITTING 1 TEN INTO 10 ONES "BREAKING" A TEN.

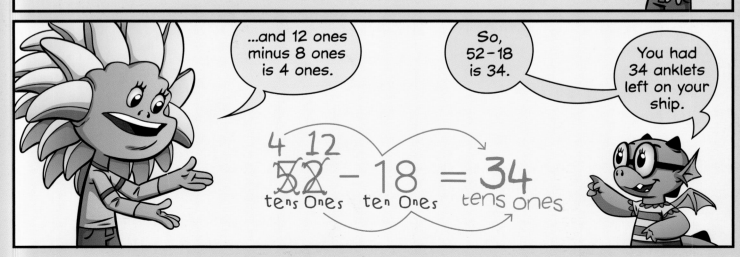

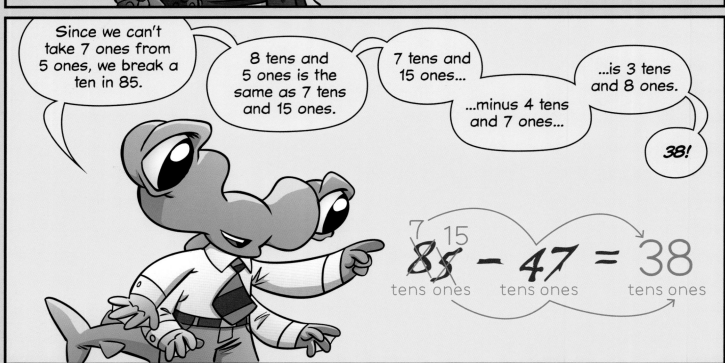

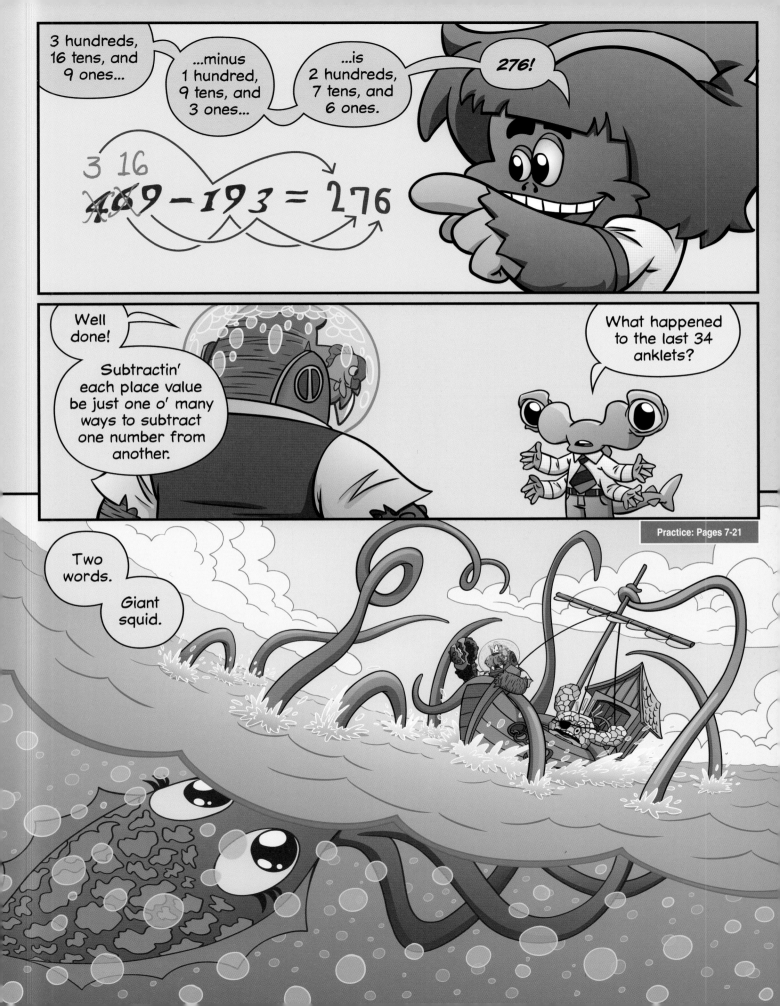

Practice: Pages 7-21

$$254 + 359 = 500 + 100 + 13 = 613$$

$$613 - 359 =$$

Try it.

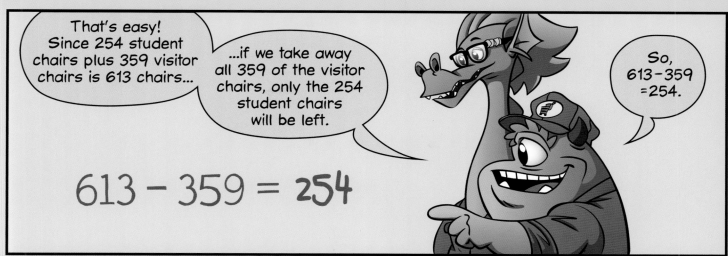

25

IN THIS BOOK, THE DIFFERENCE BETWEEN TWO NUMBERS IS THE BIGGER NUMBER MINUS THE SMALLER ONE.

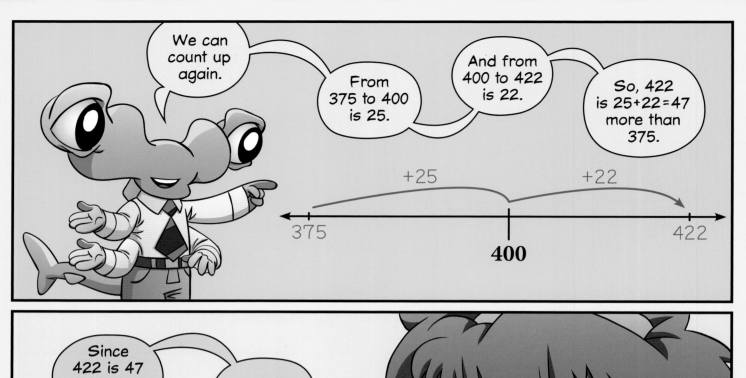

$$422 - 375 = 47$$

$$674 - 574 =$$

$$777 - 222 =$$

$$650 - 346 =$$

Try all three.

674 is 100 more than 574.

So, 674 − 574 = 100.

674 − 574 = 100

777 − 222 = 555

Taking 2 hundreds, 2 tens, and 2 ones from 777...

...we get 5 hundreds, 5 tens, and 5 ones.

To take away 346 from 650, we have to break a ten.

Counting up is easier.

From 346, we can count up by 4 to 350...

...and from 350 to 650 is 300 more.

So, 650 − 346 is 4 + 300 = **304**.

+4   +300

346   350   650

650 − 346 = 304

Or, we could count up by hundreds first to 646...

...then 4 more to 650.

We still get 304.

+100   +100   +100   +4

346   446   546   646   650

650 − 346 = 304

What is 356−198?

Practice: Pages 22-32

Subtraction Strategies

1. Place Value

$$76 - 53 = \underline{7\ 6} - \underline{5\ 3} = \underline{2\ 3}$$

tens ones   tens ones   tens ones

2. Counting Up

$$114 - 89 = 11 + 14 = 25$$

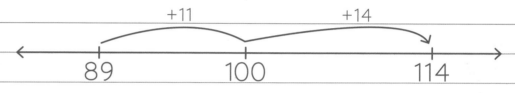

3. Subtract, then Add

$$424 - 96 = 424 - 100 + 4 = 328$$

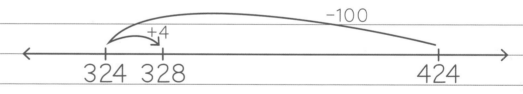

4. NEW! Shift the Difference

$$361 - 49 = 362 - 50 = 312$$

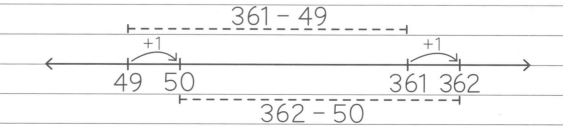

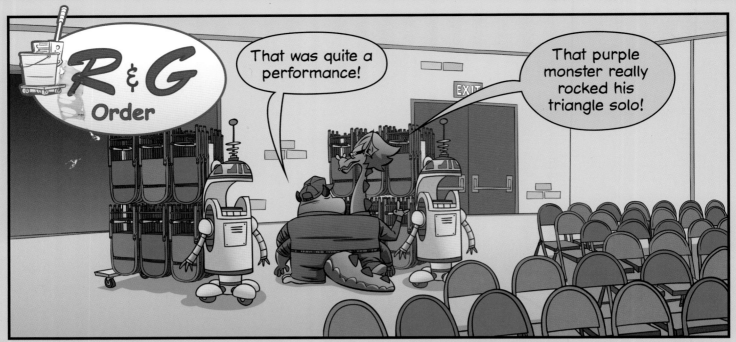

SUBTRACTING 3−5 GIVES A NEGATIVE NUMBER. YOU'LL LEARN ABOUT NEGATIVES IN BEAST ACADEMY 4C.

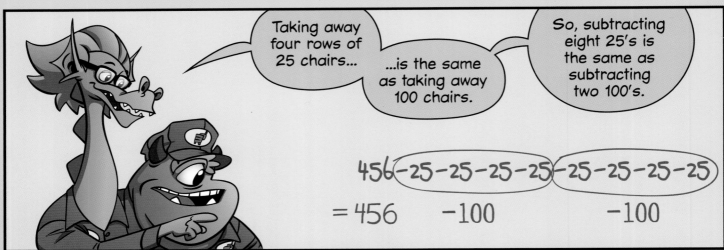

40

Practice: Pages 33-39

Contents: Chapter 5

See page 40 in the Practice book for a recommended reading/practice sequence for Chapter 5.

Ms. Q. Expressions

Who can show me a math expression?

These are the expressions I make when I do math.

These are *not* the math expressions Ms. Q. is looking for.

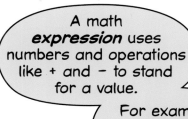
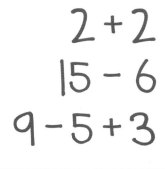

A math **expression** uses numbers and operations like + and − to stand for a value.

For example, 2+2, 15−6, and 9−5+3 are all expressions.

$$2 + 2$$
$$15 - 6$$
$$9 - 5 + 3$$

Excellent.

When we **evaluate** an expression, we find its value.

What do we get when we evaluate Lizzie's expressions?

$$2 + 2$$
$$15 - 6$$
$$9 - 5 + 3$$

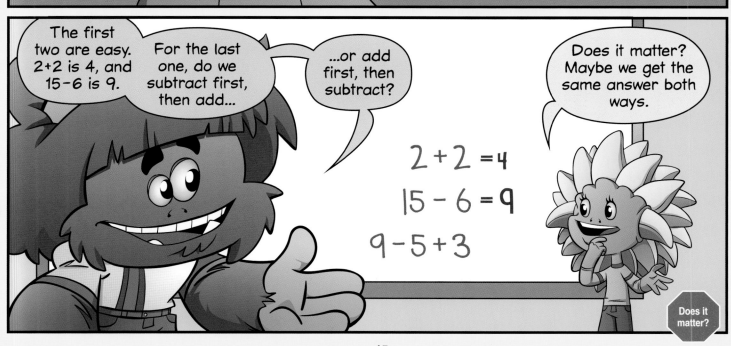

The first two are easy. 2+2 is 4, and 15−6 is 9.

For the last one, do we subtract first, then add...

...or add first, then subtract?

Does it matter? Maybe we get the same answer both ways.

$$2 + 2 = 4$$
$$15 - 6 = 9$$
$$9 - 5 + 3$$

Does it matter?

47

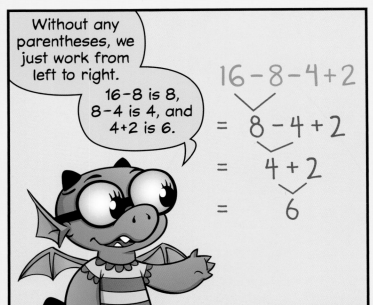

Without any parentheses, we just work from left to right.

16−8 is 8, 8−4 is 4, and 4+2 is 6.

$$16-8-4+2$$
$$= 8-4+2$$
$$= 4+2$$
$$= 6$$

We start in the parentheses for this one. 8−4=4.

Then, we work from left to right.

$$16-(8-4)+2$$
$$= 16-4+2$$
$$= 12+2$$
$$= 14$$

16−4 is 12, and 12+2 is 14.

Here, we start with 4+2=6. That gives us 16−8−6.

Then, 16−8 is 8, and 8−6 is 2.

$$16-8-(4+2)$$
$$= 16-8-6$$
$$= 8-6$$
$$= 2$$

For this one, we start in parentheses with 8−4+2.

8−4 is 4, and 4+2 is 6.

$$16-(8-4+2)$$
$$= 16-(4+2)$$
$$= 16-6$$
$$= 10$$

Then, 16−6 is 10.

Nice job. An expression can even contain more than one pair of parentheses.

How would you evaluate this one?

$$7-(5-(3-1))$$

49

I just started by writing a few different pairs of parentheses.

$$(30 - 10 + 5 - 1)$$

$$(30 - 10) + 5 - 1$$

$$(30 - 10 + 5) - 1$$

Putting parentheses around the whole expression doesn't change how we evaluate it.

We just work from left to right.

$$(30 - 10 + 5 - 1)$$
$$= 20 + 5 - 1$$
$$= 25 - 1$$
$$= 24$$

Putting parentheses around 30 − 10 doesn't change what we do first.

We subtract 30 − 10 first, with or without the parentheses.

$$(30 - 10) + 5 - 1$$
$$= 20 + 5 - 1$$
$$= 25 - 1$$
$$= 24$$

These parentheses don't change the order, either.

We get 24 again.

$$(30 - 10 + 5) - 1$$
$$= 20 + 5 - 1$$
$$= 25 - 1$$
$$= 24$$

Putting parentheses around the stuff at the **beginning** doesn't change what we do first.

Oh, right!

That stuff was going to come first, anyway!

$$(30 - 10 + 5 - 1) = 24$$
$$(30 - 10) + 5 - 1 = 24$$
$$(30 - 10 + 5) - 1 = 24$$

Maybe I'll get something different if I put the parentheses at the end, around $5 - 1$.

$$30 - 10 + (5 - 1)$$

Oh, no! I got 24 again!

The order was different, but you still got 24.

Isn't there **anywhere** I can write parentheses that **doesn't** give me 24?

$$30 - 10 + (5 - 1)$$
$$= 30 - 10 + 4$$
$$= 20 + 4$$
$$= 24$$

Can you find two more ways to place parentheses?

$(30-10)+5-1$

$30-(10+5)-1$

$30-10+(5-1)$

Let's organize all the ways to write parentheses.

There are 3 ways to group two numbers...

$(30-10+5)-1$

$30-(10+5-1)$

...2 ways to group three numbers...

$(30-10+5-1)$

...and only 1 way to group all four numbers.

$(30-10)+5-1 = 24$

$30-(10+5)-1$

$30-10+(5-1) = 24$

$(30-10+5)-1 = 24$

$30-(10+5-1)$

$(30-10+5-1) = 24$

We already evaluated four of these.

But, we haven't tried these two.

$30-(10+5)-1$

$30-(10+5-1)$

Maybe we'll get something other than 24.

Try both.

53

...41 pushups!

$$\square + 10$$
$$= 31 + 10$$
$$= 41$$

dab dab dab

Yep. We're gonna look awesome!

Next is jogging.

The poster says that we jog for ☆-40 minutes.

What does ☆ stand for?

☆-40
minutes

☆ stands for the day's high temperature.

It's supposed to get up to 65 today.

Yep. So, how many minutes do we have to jog?

☆-40

How many?

58

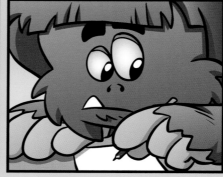

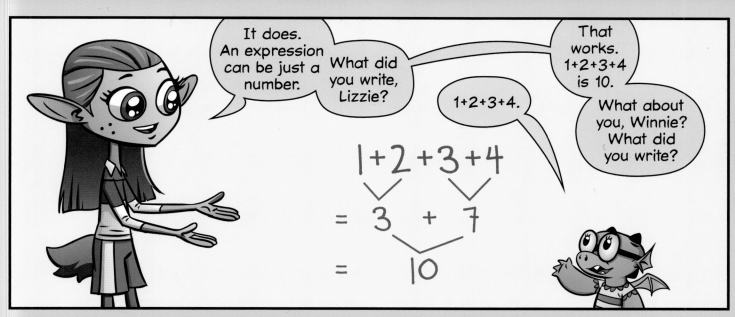

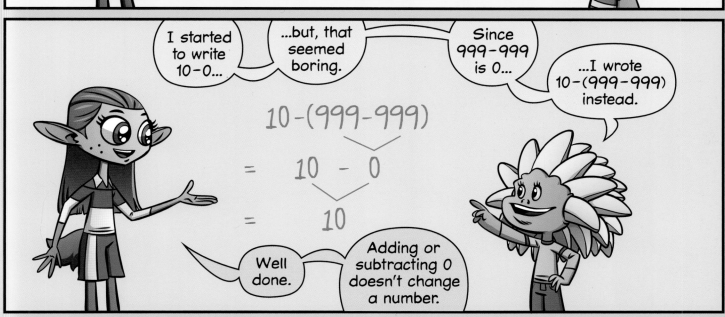

61

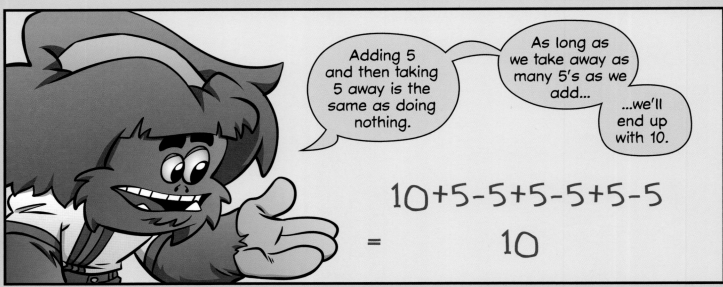

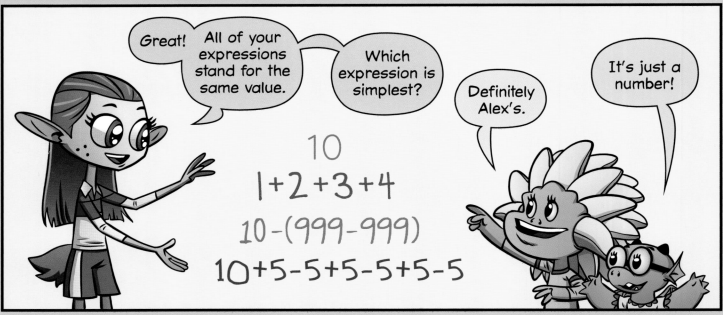

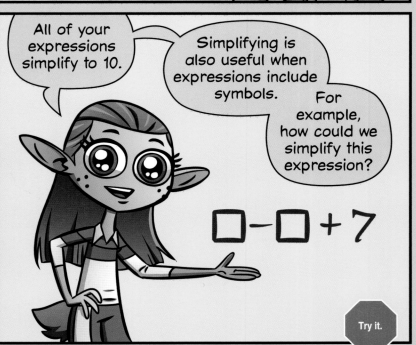

What does the □ stand for?

It doesn't matter!

Huh?

The first thing we do is subtract □−□.

$$\square - \square + 7$$
$$= \quad 0 + 7$$
$$= \quad 7$$

1−1 is 0.
50−50 is 0.
999−999 is 0.
Any number minus itself is 0.

So, no matter what number □ is, □−□ is *always* 0.

So, □−□+7 is *always* 7.

That means □−□+7 *simplifies* to 7.

That's right. What about this one?

How could you simplify △+6−6?

$$\triangle + 6 - 6$$

Try it.

63

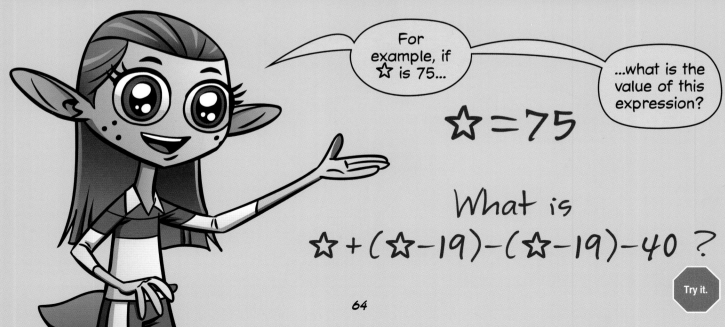

Panel 1

"We can replace every ☆ with 75."

$$☆ + (☆ − 19) − (☆ − 19) − 40 \ ?$$
$$= 75 + (75 − 19) − (75 − 19) − 40$$
$$= 75 + 56 − 56 − 40$$

"Then, we do what's in parentheses."

"75−19 is 56."

Panel 2

"Adding 56 then subtracting 56 is the same as doing nothing."

$$☆ + (☆ − 19) − (☆ − 19) − 40 \ ?$$
$$= 75 + (75 − 19) − (75 − 19) − 40$$
$$= 75 \ \cancel{56} \quad \cancel{56} \ − 40$$

"So, we can just cross these out."

Panel 3

"That leaves us with 75−40..." "...which is **35!**"

$$☆ + (☆ − 19) − (☆ − 19) − 40 \ ?$$
$$= 75 + (75 − 19) − (75 − 19) − 40$$
$$= 75 \ \cancel{56} \quad \cancel{56} \ − 40$$
$$= \quad 75 − 40$$
$$= \quad 35$$

"Well done."

Panel 4

"What does the same expression give us when ☆ is 54?"

$$☆ = 54$$
$$☆ + (☆ − 19) − (☆ − 19) − 40$$

"Maybe we can simplify **before** we replace all of the ☆'s."

"Can you simplify the expression?"

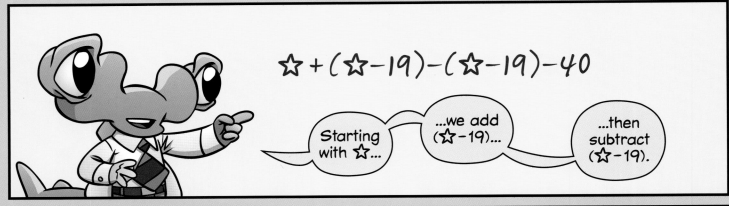

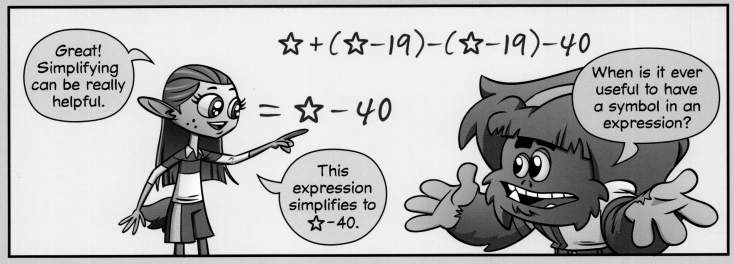

To figure out what number the 🌙 stands for...

...we need to know what number plus 3 equals 30.

$$🌙 + 3 = 30$$
$$\_ + 3 = 30$$

Since *27*+3 = 30...

...the 🌙 stands for 27.

$$🌙 + 3 = 30$$
$$\underline{27} + 3 = 30$$

Aye, there be 27 moonstones in this chest.

Findin' the value o' a symbol in an equation be called **solving** the equation.

🌙 + 3 = 30

Next, try solving the equation on this chest. The heart stands for the number o' heartcoins within.

How many heartcoins be there?

$$10 + 40 = ❤ + 30$$

How many?

70

On the left side of the equation, we have 10+40, which equals 50.

$$10 + 40 = ♥ + 30$$
$$50 =$$

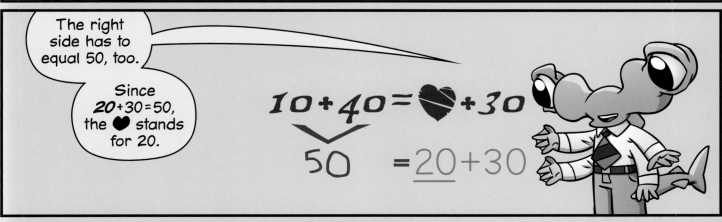

The right side has to equal 50, too.

Since 20+30=50, the ♥ stands for 20.

$$10 + 40 = ♥ + 30$$
$$50 = \underline{20} + 30$$

So, there are 20 heartcoins.

Well done!

In the third chest, there be skull rings.

The skull symbol stands for the number o' rings in the chest.

This time, we have symbols on both sides o' the equation.

What number does 💀 stand for?

$$💀 + (💀 - 5) = 💀 + 12$$

Try it.

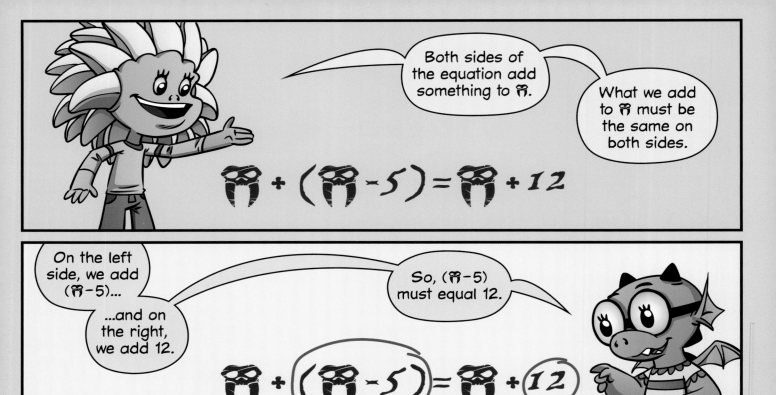

Contents: Chapter 6

See page 72 in the Practice book for a recommended reading/practice sequence for Chapter 6.

Chapter 6:
Problem Solving

77

83

84

Practice: Pages 82-89

Very good, Grogg.

Sometimes, a drawing can be very helpful for solving a problem.

How could drawing a picture help you solve *this* problem?

Sam is 3 years older than Tom, who is 1 year older than Ron. Pam is 2 years older than Tom, but 2 years younger than Quinn.

Sam, Tom, Ron, Quinn, and Pam line up from youngest to oldest. Who stands in the middle?

I'll draw Sam.

He's going to have a cool superhero cape and a mask.

You do not need to *draw* all five monsters, Grogg! We can just write an "S" to stand for Sam.

Who stands in the middle?

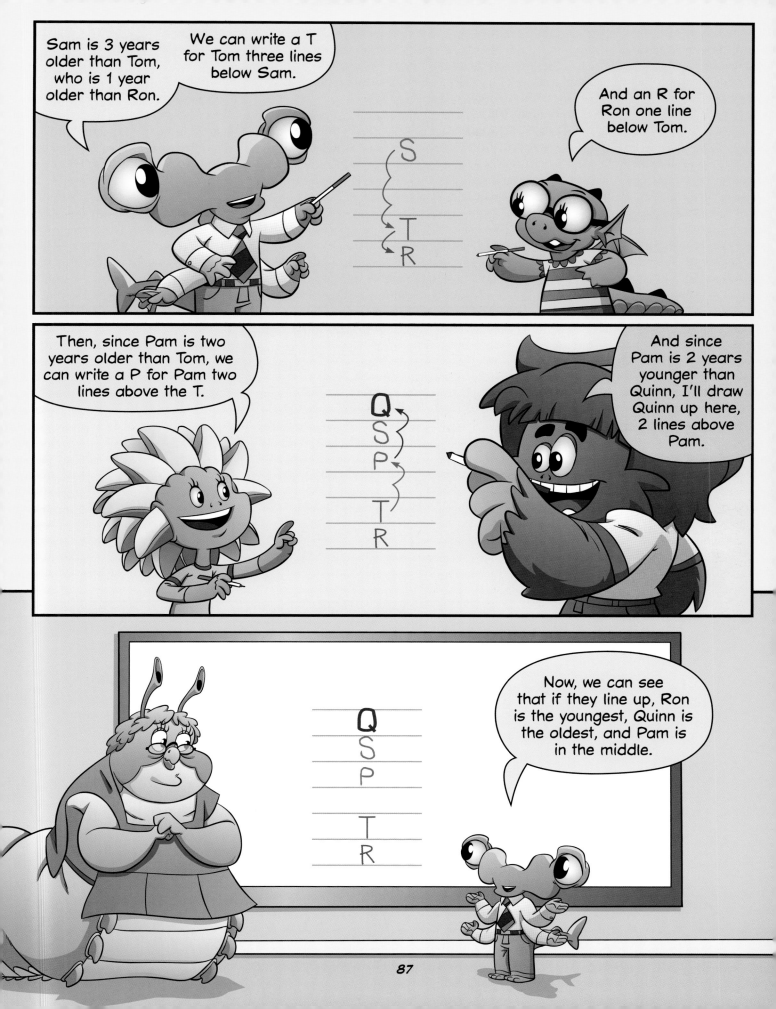

Five teams are in a beastball league. Each team plays every other team once. How many games are played all together?

702 pounds.

I'm sorry, that is incorrect.

The question didn't ask for Borg's weight... ...just what day he weighed himself the second time.

He first weighed himself on Tuesday, then again 10 days later.

Seven days later, it would be Tuesday again.

And three days after that would be...

ding!

...Friday!

Su M Tu W Th F Sa

Friday is correct! The little monsters score the first point.

Question 2:
Jenny, Kenny, and Lenny all live in different houses on Yeti Lane. There are three houses between Jenny's and Kenny's, and three houses between Kenny's and Lenny's. How many houses are between Jenny's and Lenny's?

Try it.

94

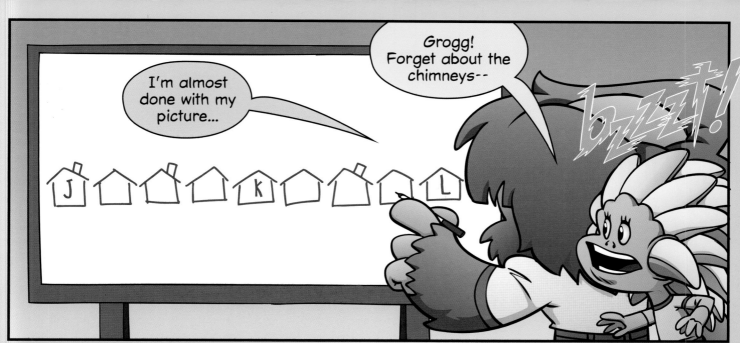

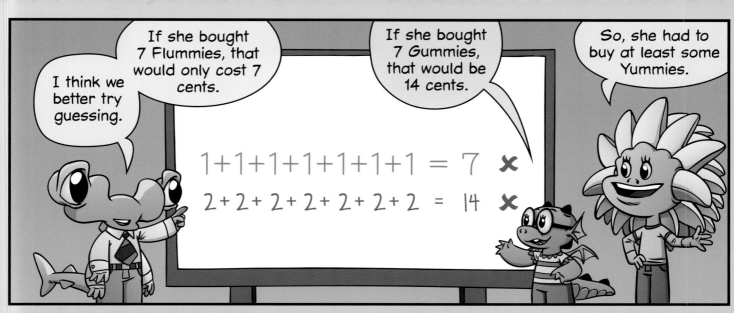

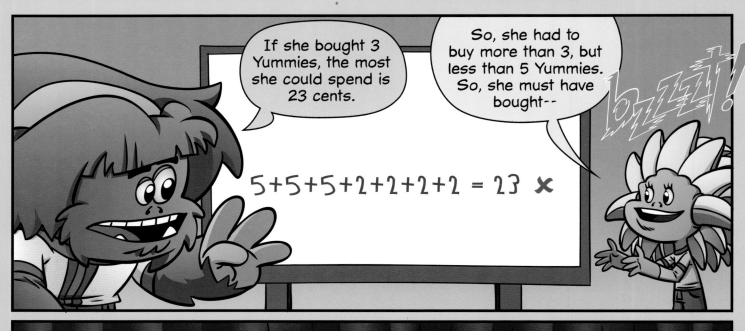

We can work backwards.

When the third car drove by, half of the birds left, but two came back.

That left 7 birds in the tree.

So, before the two birds came back, there were just 7−2=5 birds in the tree.

VRRROOOOOOOM

And before the third car scared half the birds away, there were 5+5=10 birds in the tree.

Now, we can figure out how many birds there were before the second car drove by.

The second car scared half of the birds, but two came back.

So, before the two birds came back, there were just 10−2=8 birds in the tree.

ZOOM ZOOM

And before the second car scared half of them off, there were 8+8=16 birds in the tree.

Finish the problem.

99

The first car scared half the birds, but two came back. So, before two birds came back, there were 16 − 2 = 14 birds in the tree.

And before the first car scared half the birds away...

Rumble Rumble

There were 14 + 14 = ...

bzzzt!

28 elefinches.

28 is correct! The score is now Bots: 3, Little Monsters: 2.

Remember, the last question is worth 2 points.

Oh, no! We were so close!

We need to get the last question right to beat the bots.

Question 6:
Ayana sold a total of 100 cups of lemonade on Thursday, Friday, Saturday, and Sunday. She sold 2 more cups on Friday than she sold on Thursday. She sold twice as many cups on Saturday as she sold on Friday. On Sunday, she sold as many cups as she sold on the other three days combined. How many cups did she sell on Sunday?

Try it.

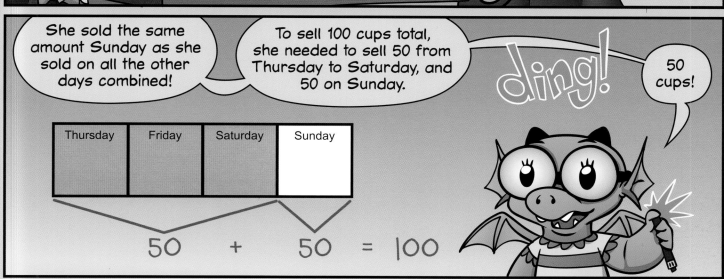

Index

For additional books,
printables, and more, visit
BeastAcademy.com